DIVINE POWER

Stuff- The material out of which anything is made

Produced and Published by Infinite Generations
137 National Plaza, Suite 300
National Harbor, MD 20745
1-(855)-455-0125
www.infinitegenerations.com

ISBN:
978-1-953364-76-0 (Paperback)

Printed in the United States of America
First Printing, 2025

Divine Power

NO ONE LOSES WITH THE STUFF GOD USES

Infinite Generations Publishing
Faith Word Healing Books

Dedication

This book is lovingly dedicated to my grandmother, Everlena, a woman of wisdom, strength, and unwavering faith. She deeply believed in the power of God's creation and the blessings found in living off the land. As a child growing up I remember her having the land harvest during different seasons of the year planting all kinds of food and healing herbs. Those were the best times of my childhood, as I look back today and see how important it is to live off the land.

One of her favorite scriptures, Genesis 1:29, "I have given you every herb bearing seed." She loved living off the land and growing just about every plant and healing herb in the bible. There were maple, dandelion, longan, persimmon, apple, pear, and cherry trees. These trees, were used for food or medicine. Also, there were grapes, plums, walnuts, and blackberries. Each year when the cane and wheat was ready to be processed they were sent to the Mill. The cane came back as molasses in glass jars; and the wheat came back in sacks as flour. During the winter season she was a strong believer in using the onions from her garden to treat our head cold, body aches, temperature and flu. Whatever illness came her way, she had home grown remedies for treatment. Today, I continue to use those recipes for healthy cooking and healing. Thank you Grandma. You will always be in my heart.

Love you,
Carrie

Author's Note

I wrote this book with one purpose on my heart—to remind you that God is our source and miracles still happen.

Too often, we overlook the everyday elements God uses to reveal His extraordinary power. Whether it's water, wind, oil, light, or even a handful of loaves and fish, our God has always used natural things to produce supernatural outcomes. And the best part? He still does.

This book is more than stories and scriptures—it's a testimony. A testimony that God is not done. His power is alive, and His presence is near. I wanted to share the "stuff" God uses, the things that are often right in front of us, to show that His wonder-working power hasn't faded. He still heals, still provides, still comforts, and still breaks chains.

My prayer is that as you read these pages, your faith is stirred, your eyes are opened, and your spirit is renewed. May you begin to recognize the miraculous in the mundane—and believe again that nothing is impossible for God.

With faith and gratitude,

Rev. Dr. Carrie M. Spruill

Introduction

God is almighty, all-knowing, and ever-present. He has the power to do what He wants, how He wants, and when He wants—Divine Power has always amazed believers throughout time.

When a miracle is performed, it is God's way of revealing evidence of His Divine Power. Some may claim that miracles only happened during biblical times and are no longer active today. But the truth is: miracles are still happening every single day.

Scientists define miracles as mysterious or unusual events that defy the laws of nature. That's because miracles come from a divine source—a God whose power is the origin of nature itself. He is the God who stepped out of nowhere, formed the earth out of nothing, and hung it on nothing—what we now refer to as gravity.

This is the evidence of a divine God at work.

Our Heavenly Father uses different kinds of "stuff"—tools, elements, and ordinary things—as ways to demonstrate His extraordinary power. In fact, what we often consider simple or insignificant can be the very things God uses to build our courage, confidence, and dependence on Him. Scripture constantly encourages us to live with bold faith, stand strong in confidence, and trust fully in the Lord.

In the Old Testament, God used dust to create mankind and used countless other natural elements to perform miracles. In the New Testament, His Son, Jesus Christ, walked the earth for 33 years, performing miracle after miracle—starting with turning water into wine at a wedding. And today, as Jesus sits at the right hand of the Father, miracles continue to unfold here on earth.

This book is titled, "Divine Power: The Stuff God Uses", because throughout scripture, we see how God works through ordinary means to accomplish extraordinary things. From mud and spit to wind and water, He has shown us that His power is not limited by the material—but glorified through it.

God tells us in His Word that we must have faith and believe. In Matthew 17:20, Jesus says:

> "Because of your unbelief: for verily I say unto you, If ye have faith as a grain of mustard seed, ye shall say unto this mountain, Remove hence to yonder place; and it shall remove; and nothing shall be impossible unto you."

This book highlights the "stuff" and means God uses—then and now—to awaken faith in both believers and unbelievers. May these pages open your eyes to the divine power of God, encourage your spirit, and strengthen your belief that miracles still happen.

Acknowledgements

This book would not have been possible without the extraordinary people who strongly support me.

First, I thank God for giving me the knowledge to write.

Thanks to my husband, Elijah, who consistently shows patience and understanding while I am writing.

Thanks to my daughter, India, who helps to organize and edit most of my books. She firmly believes the books I write will empower and benefit many people.

Of course, none of this would have been possible without the full support of Infinite Generations Publishers. The team showed faith in helping pull this book together, and I am grateful to them.

Finally, I want to thank everyone who will take the time to read and share this book with others.

Contents

Contents

I

The Power of Creation

"For through him God created everything in the heavenly realms and on earth. He made the things we can see and the things we can't see... Everything was created through him and for him."

–Colossians 1:16

In The Beginning

"In the beginning was the Word, and the Word was with God and the Word was God."
John 1:1

This teaches us that Jesus Christ existed before the world was created and is God Himself. The Word became flesh in the New Testament through the virgin Mary.

God is Spirit

"God is spirit, without flesh and blood and invisible." - John 4:24

The nature of God transcends the physical realm. Unlike man, who is bound by time, space, and matter, God is eternal, limitless, and invisible— yet fully present in all things. This divine truth reminds us that our connection with Him must go beyond rituals or physical places. It is a relationship rooted in faith, truth, and spiritual awareness.

According to Isaiah 66:1, Heaven is His home and earth is His footstool.

Seven Days of Creation

Day One

"Let there be light." - Genesis 1:3

In that moment, light broke through the void, illuminating creation with divine brilliance. This was no ordinary light—it was the first evidence of God's power moving across the deep. Before the sun, moon, or stars were formed, God established the principle of separation: light from darkness. This was more than just physical light; it was symbolic of the spiritual clarity, truth, and presence that only God can bring. In creating light, He introduced hope, direction, and the beginning of time itself.

From the very first day, God revealed His authority to transform chaos into order, and darkness into purpose. His light became the foundation for all creation and remains a spiritual metaphor for His presence in our lives. Just as He separated the light from darkness in the beginning, He continues to call us out of spiritual darkness into His marvelous light (1 Peter 2:9). Day One is a reminder that no matter how deep the darkness may seem in our lives, one word from God is enough to bring light, clarity, and a new beginning. The same power that lit the universe now lives in us.

Day Two

On the second day of creation, God spoke again—and the skies were born. According to Genesis 1:6-8, God created a vast expanse to separate the waters above from the waters below. He called this expanse "sky." In this divine act, God not only formed the atmosphere that would sustain life but also displayed His perfect order and wisdom. The sky acts as a protective covering over the earth, regulating weather, giving us breathable air, and painting daily reminders of His glory with sunrises, sunsets, and starry nights.

What may seem ordinary to us—clouds drifting, rain falling, the breeze blowing—is actually a supernatural system held together by God's hand. Day two reminds us that even the invisible layers of life, like the air we breathe, are evidence of His care, creativity, and control.

Day Three

Genesis 1:9-10, talks about the sea,

"And God said, Let the waters under the heavens be gathered together into one place, and let the dry land appear."

And it was so. God called the dry land Earth, and the waters that were gathered together He called Seas. And God saw that it was good."

God prepared a good land and gave mankind every kind of herb and seed needed for nourishment. Deuteronomy 8:8,

"And God said, let the earth bring forth the green herb, and such as may seed, and the fruit tree yielding fruit after its kind, which may have seed in itself upon the earth. And it was done."

Day Four

On the fourth day of creation, God placed lights in the heavens with intentional care and purpose. Genesis 1:14-19 tells us that He created the sun to govern the day, the moon to rule the night, and the stars to mark sacred times and seasons.

Our Heavenly Father, in His infinite wisdom, gave mankind everything needed to survive and thrive. The sun provides warmth and energy, making it possible for plants to grow and life to flourish. The moon gently lights the darkness and helps regulate the ocean tides—guiding rhythms of rest, growth, and renewal.

These celestial bodies are not only functional but also beautiful reminders of God's precision, power, and provision. Day four shows us that God doesn't just create—He sustains. Every sunrise and moonlit night is a testimony of His faithful care, shining down on a world He lovingly formed.

Day Five

Genesis 1:20–23

On the fifth day of creation, God spoke, and the skies and seas came alive.

"And God said, 'Let the waters swarm with swarms of living creatures, and let birds fly above the earth across the expanse of the heavens.' So God created the great sea creatures and every living creature that moves, with which the waters swarm, according to their kinds, and every winged bird according to its kind. From the depths of the oceans to the heights of the heavens, God filled His creation with movement, sound, color, and wonder.

But more than a display of beauty, Day 5 reminds us of God's intentional design. He did not just create birds and sea creatures randomly—He made them according to their kind, with purpose, instinct, and role. Every detail was spoken into existence by His Word and held together by His power.

The same God who created the mighty whale and the delicate hummingbird also formed you—with just as much care and intention.

This day in creation speaks of God's ability to fill the void with life. Where there was once only water and sky, now there is abundance. He is still the God who fills—He fills our empty spaces, our hearts, our hopes—with His Spirit and divine presence.

And God saw that it was good.

Day Six

According to Genesis 2:7, God formed man from the dust of the ground and breathed into his nostrils the breath of life, making him a living being. Without the breath of God man formed out of dust would not be alive. Therefore, man has a spiritual nature which connects with the body and soul. At the time of death, the body goes back into the earth as dust, and the spirit goes to a place that has been prepared. If we are believers, the breath He breathed into us will return back to him. This means we shall dwell with Him forever. For unbelievers, the spirit goes away from the presence of the Heavenly Father.

"God created man in his own image,
in the image of God created he him;
male and female created he them."
-Genesis 1:27-28

Gensis 2:18-23, tells us after God created Adam He said it was not good for man to be alone. Therefore, out of the ground He formed every beast of the field and fowl of the air and asked Adam to name them; but there was no help mate for Adam. Scripture says, God caused Adam to go into a deep sleep and removed a rib out of him and formed woman and named her Eve. Scripture also tells us that God used dust from the earth to create animals. He called the first man and woman, Adam and Eve. He asked Adam to name all the animals.

Day Seven

On the seventh day, God completed His masterpiece. The heavens, the earth, the stars, the waters, and every living creature had been spoken into existence. And with divine satisfaction, the Creator paused—not because He was tired, but because the work was whole, complete, and perfectly good. Genesis 2:2-3 says,

"By the seventh day God had finished the work He had been doing; so on the seventh day He rested from all His work. Then God blessed the seventh day and made it holy."

God's rest set a precedent, not just for physical renewal, but for spiritual rhythm. It reminds us that in a world of constant motion, rest is not weakness—it is worship. Rest is an act of trust in the One who holds all things together. Even today, God invites us into His rest. In Matthew 11:28, Jesus extends a divine invitation: "Come to me, all who are weary and burdened, and I will give you rest." In His finished work, we find peace.

May we learn to pause, breathe, and rest—knowing that the God who created the universe also cares deeply for us. His work is finished. His power is eternal. And His rest is still available for all who believe.

The Garden of Eden

The garden of Eden is where God placed first man and woman to live and fellowship with Him. He created the first woman by taking a rib from Adam to be his helper. Scripture tells us it was a perfect place filled with plants, trees, rivers and animals which Adam named. Adam and Eve was to cultivate it and live the perfect life without sin. There were two trees, the tree of life and the tree of the knowledge of good and evil. They were told not to eat from the tree of knowledge of good and evil, but instead they listened to the serpent which was satan; they ate from the tree. This caused sin and death to enter into the world. God expelled Adam and Eve from the garden. Therefore, mankind continues to live in sin. Although, the serpent caused man to fall, but because of God's goodness and mercy He found a way to bridge the gap and bring mankind back into compliance with Him Genesis 3:15 through the seed of a woman.

I Have Given You Everything

"I have given you every plant yielding seed which is upon the face of all the earth, and every tree with seed in its fruit; you shall have them for food."
-Genesis 1:29

As we look around us in modern time today we realize the importance of the stuff God created for us to eat.

Modern times has gotten away from using or eating the Healing food God intended for mankind. In today's world our food supply has changed, therefore the food God intended for our bodies is not in its original form after being over processed or other artificial ingredients added.

Healthy Anti-Aging Foods

According to Genesis Chapters 5 and 11, people in biblical times lived significantly longer than we do today. Adam lived to be 930 years old, and Methuselah reached 969 years. One key difference was their diet—food came directly from the earth in its purest, unprocessed form. In contrast, today's heavily processed foods are filled with artificial ingredients that our bodies struggle to digest, contributing to chronic illness and accelerated aging.

In Numbers 11:5, the children of Israel longed for the foods they once ate in Egypt: fish, cucumbers, melons, leeks, onions, and garlic. These natural, nutrient-rich foods weren't just flavorful—they were also healing. For example, onions are known to help lower cholesterol and reduce fever, aches, and cold symptoms. Garlic, closely related to the onion, has been celebrated for its immune-boosting and anti-inflammatory properties.

Leeks, a milder and slightly sweeter cousin to the onion, were also used for flavor and healing. Melons, similar to today's cantaloupe, are rich in vitamins A, C, and B6—all powerful nutrients that support healthy skin, vision, and the immune system, making them effective anti-aging foods. Fish, both in biblical times and today, remains a vital source of Omega-3 fatty acids, which support heart health, reduce inflammation, and protect the brain from age-related decline.

Perhaps one of the most powerful biblical healing foods is the olive. Mentioned throughout scripture, olives and olive oil were used for cooking, healing, and anointing. Rich in antioxidants and healthy fats, olive oil is still known today for moisturizing skin, reducing wrinkles, and promoting cardiovascular health.

And while apples are often linked to the Garden of Eden, the Bible never actually names them as the forbidden fruit. Nevertheless, in today's world, apples are considered a superfood, with their fiber and antioxidant content promoting digestion, detoxification, and longevity.

These biblical foods are not just historically significant—they are still some of the most powerful anti-aging and healing foods available today. By returning to the natural diet God originally gave us, we can reclaim health, vitality, and long life.

Healing through God's Creation

Throughout Scripture and still today, we see that healing flows through God's creation. From the plants and herbs of the earth to the water that refreshes and restores, God has designed nature with divine purpose. In Genesis, every element created was declared "good," and within that goodness is healing—both physical and spiritual. He used clay to restore sight, spoke to winds and waves to bring peace, and instructed prophets to use natural remedies for wellness. God's creation is not random; it's intentional.

His power is woven into the earth, the sky, and every living thing. Healing through creation is just one way He reveals His love, reminding us that the same God who formed the universe also formed the path to our restoration.

II

Man's Journey and Redemption

"Not by might, nor by power, but by my Spirit, says the Lord of hosts."
- Zechariah 4:6

Restoration by Faith

Leviticus 14 outlines a powerful and symbolic ritual for the purification of a person healed from leprosy. In this divine instruction, God commanded the use of two birds, fresh water, and other elements in a sacred act of restoration. One bird was sacrificed over running water, while the other was dipped into the blood and then released into the open fields. This act was rich in meaning—one bird representing the cost of cleansing, and the other symbolizing freedom, new life, and restored wholeness.

Through this ritual, God didn't just offer physical healing—He gave the people something tangible to see and believe in. The ceremony stirred their faith and revealed His divine power at work. It was a visible reminder that healing is not only possible but purposeful. God used the "stuff" of earth—birds, water, and blood—to represent His grace, to strengthen their faith, and to show that restoration always begins with Him.

Crossing the Impossible

Exdous 3:9-11 tell us God sent Moses into Egypt to deliver His people, the children of Israel out of Egypt. Moses asked God, who must I say sent me, God answered and said, "Say unto them IAM hath sent me unto you."

Exodous 14:21-23 says, Moses and the children of Israel fled Egypt with Pharoah right on their trail. When they reached the Red Sea Moses stretched out his hand over the sea; and the LORD caused the sea to go back by a strong east wind all that night, and made the sea into dry land, and the waters were divided. So the children of Israel went into the midst of the sea and the land that was once water in the floor of the sea is now dry land. The children of Israel walked out on dry land from the sea and was saved from the Egyptians.

Scripture says the water returned back to the sea causing Pharoah and his army to drown in the midst of the Red Sea.

Provision in the Wilderness

In 1 Kings 17:1–6, we find the powerful and humbling story of the prophet Elijah being fed by ravens—a clear example of God's divine provision in the midst of drought and uncertainty. After Elijah boldly declared a drought upon the land as directed by God, the Lord instructed him to hide by the brook Cherith.

There, God promised to supply his needs in an unexpected way: by commanding ravens to bring him bread and meat each morning and evening. True to His word, God used these unlikely messengers—unclean birds by tradition—to sustain Elijah during a time of scarcity. This miraculous provision not only demonstrates God's power over nature but also His faithfulness to provide for His people in the most surprising and supernatural ways.

It reminds us that no matter how desolate the season, God can send provision from places we'd never expect.

Our God is sovereign and will supply all our needs.
Just as He did for Elijah when there was a draught in the land.
While hiding down by the Brook of Cherith with no food in sight,
Elijah became hungry. God sent a raven to supply him
with breakfast, lunch and dinner.

The Messiah Foretold

According to Isaiah 7:14, the Lord himself will give a sign, therefore a virgin shall conceive and bear a son, and shall call his name Immanuel.

Isaiah 53, describes the Messiah's suffering and death as a sacrifice for the sins of humanity.

III

Miracles and Jesus' Healing Power

"Jesus looked at them and said, "With man this is impossible, but with God all things are possible.""
– Matthew 19:26

The Gift of Hope is Born

"For unto us a child is born, unto us a son is given: and the government shall be upon his shoulder: and his name shall be called Wonderful, Counsellor, The mighty God, The everlasting Father, The Prince of Peace."

Isaiah 9:6

Our Father gave mankind the most precious gift we can ever receive.

In Him we find HOPE, we find JOY, we find PEACE through the power of the Holy Spirit because we are faithful believers.

Yes, this precious gift was given to us and we know Him as Wonderful, our Counsellor, The mighty God, and The everlasting Father. Although, He is The Prince of Peace – we realize that this world is still in need of Peace, but the good news is that there will be peace on earth when He returns to build His Kingdom.

The first time He arrived on Christmas Day, a star marked His arrival. The next time He arrives heaven will open up, and all the stars will fall from the sky, and He Himself will be the light.

It is alright to exchange gifts on this Day because gifts were exchanged when Christ was born. The Three Wise Men gave gifts to baby Jesus (Matthew 2:9-11). It is not all about the gifts we receive under the tree -- it is about the gift that died on the tree for our sins and gave us the gift of eternal life.

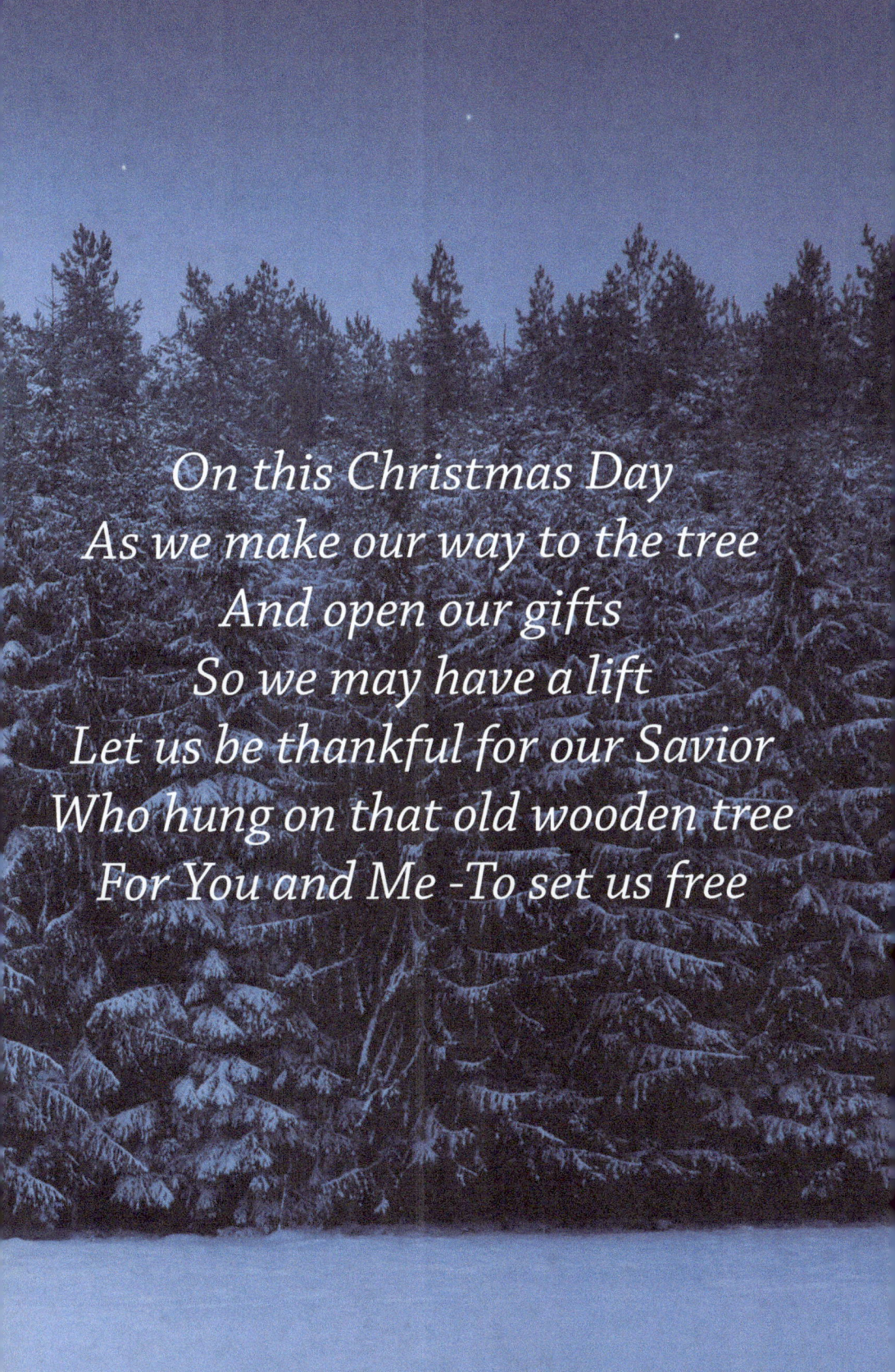

On this Christmas Day
As we make our way to the tree
And open our gifts
So we may have a lift
Let us be thankful for our Savior
Who hung on that old wooden tree
For You and Me -To set us free

Jesus Childhood and Ministry

Luke 2:41-52, tells us Jesus attended a Passover Feast with His parents in Jerusalem. As the parents were returning back home to Nazareth Jesus was missing. After looking for Him, Jesus was found in the temple discussing the Word of God with the teacher. His parents rebuked him, and Jesus replied,

"Didn't you know I had to be in my Father's house?"

This response shows that during His childhood, Jesus knew God was using Him to save mankind.

Jesus Baptized

According to Matthew 3:13–17, Jesus was baptized by John the Baptist in the Jordan River. This event, recorded in all four Gospels, is more than a historical moment; it is a divine declaration of identity, purpose, and power.

As Jesus came up out of the water, the heavens opened, and the Spirit of God descended like a dove, resting upon Him. Then came a voice from heaven declaring,

"This is my beloved Son, in whom I am well pleased."

This divine moment marked the beginning of Jesus' public ministry. Scripture reveals that He was in His early thirties when He stepped fully into His calling—ushering in miracles, healing, and a message of hope that would transform the world.

Jesus First
Miracle
*Turning Water
to Wine*

Jesus attended a wedding at Cana of Galilee, along with His disciples, mother and brothers.

"And when they wanted wine the mother of Jesus saith unto him they have no wine." (John 2:3)

"Jesus saith unto her, Woman, what have I to do with thee? mine hour is not yet come." (John 2:4)

"His mother, saith unto the servants, Whatsoever he saith unto you, do it." (John 2:5)

Now Jesus is preparing to work a miracle. There were six waterpots and,

"Jesus saith unto them fill the waterpots with water."

Most people want to know why did Jesus need six waterpots? Why did He ask for water? And why would Jesus turn water to wine? Isn't wine something Jesus should not use or give to others. These are excellent questions to ask because the bible gives us the answers.

The waterpots were made of stone hewn out of rock. Psalm 18:2, "The Lord is my rock," the rock symbolizes the Lord who is the rock of our salvation where the Holy Spirit dwells without measure; six is the number of man, and the last day all things were created. Jesus commanded the six waterpots to be filled with water,

"That he might sanctify and cleanse it with the washing of water by the word."
-Ephesians 5:26

In the New Testament, Jesus uses wine to signify the New Covenant in Jesus' blood.

Jesus Healing with Nature

In the most unexpected ways, Jesus revealed that healing was not about glamour or grandeur—it was about divine power meeting human need.

In Mark 8:22–26, we witness Jesus spitting on the eyes of a blind man, and his sight is restored. Again, in John 9:6–7, He spits on the ground, makes mud with His hands, and anoints the eyes of another blind man, who is then miraculously healed. And in Mark 7:32–35, Jesus touches the tongue of a man who could neither hear nor speak, using His own saliva—and the man's speech and hearing are instantly restored.

These sacred, earthy acts remind us that God can use the simplest elements—dust, spit, touch—to release His supernatural power.

Through what others may see as common, Jesus performed the extraordinary. This chapter explores the humility, intentionality, and spiritual significance behind these moments, proving that no method is too small or too strange for the miracle-working hand of God.

When Little Becomes More

Jesus feeding 5,000 people with two fish and five loaves of bread

The miraculous feeding of the 5,000 is one of the most powerful demonstrations of Jesus' compassion and divine power. Found in all four Gospels, this moment captures how Jesus took two fish and five loaves of bread—offered by a young boy—and multiplied them to feed a massive crowd of hungry people (Matthew 14:13–21).

What seemed small and insignificant in the hands of man became more than enough in the hands of the Savior.

Not only did everyone eat and become full, but twelve baskets of leftovers remained, symbolizing God's abundant provision. This miracle reminds us that no matter how little we have, when we give it to God in faith, He can turn it into overflow. It is a testament to His divine ability to meet both our spiritual and physical needs.

Man with Dropsy

Luke 14:1-6, Scripture tells us as Jesus went into a house on Sabbath day to eat bread where there was a man with dropsy who wanted to be healed. Jesus was questioned by the lawyers and Pharisees about healing on Sabbath day.

Jesus answered by saying,
   "Is it lawful to heal on the sabbath day?"

Scripture tells us that Jesus healed the man of dropsy. According to the word divine healing can take place any where, time or day.

A Woman with an issue of Blood

The (Gospel of Luke 8:43-48), tells the story of a woman with an issue of blood who had been sick for a long time. Upon hearing that Jesus was coming to town, she put a demand on His anointing and made her way to where He stood in the crowd. Jesus felt the powerful demand of her faith drawing the anointing out of Him and said, "who touched me?" She was healed instantly! This same healing is offered to us today, but first we must draw from the reservoir of anointing. Every time Jesus performed a miracle there was a healing. Whatever our needs are the Lord will supply, if only we believe. Our Lord and Savior is the same yesterday and today. What was done for the people then, will be done for us today. Because of His faithfulness we can trust that He will always be with us. It does not matter what our circumstances are – our Savior is still in control.

"And Jesus went about all Galilee, teaching in their synagogues, preaching the gospel of the kingdom, and healing all manner of sickness and all manner of diseases among the people."
Matthew 4:23

Every sickness, and needs of the people who came to Jesus was healed because they put a demand on His supply of anointing. All believers have been offered the anointing assured by the Cross.

Lazarus

According to John 11: 1-45, Jesus was a friend of Mary and Martha. When word got to him their brother Lazarus was sick, Jesus replied,
"This sickness is not unto death, but for the glory of God, that the Son of God might be glorified thereby."

When Jesus arrived Mary fell on her knees crying and told Jesus if He had been there her brother would not have died. Jesus asked to be taken where Lazarus had been laid. Lazarus sister Martha told Jesus Lazarus had been dead for four day and now he stinketh. Jesus asked for the stone to be removed where Lazarus laid and lift up His eyes and said, "Father I thank thee that thou hast heard me. And I know that thou hearest me always but because of the people which stand by I said it, that they may believe that thou hast sent me." After speaking those words Jesus called out,
"Lazarus, come forth."

The word tells us that he that was dead came forth.

Jesus Commandment of Love

Among all the miracles Jesus performed and all the lessons He taught, one message stood above the rest—love. Not just any love, but a divine, transformative, all-encompassing love that has the power to heal hearts, restore relationships, and change the world. In John 13:34, Jesus said, "A new command I give you: Love one another. As I have loved you, so you must love one another." This was no suggestion. It was a charge to carry divine power in our hearts and express it in our actions.

Jesus didn't just teach love—He lived it. He healed the sick out of compassion, forgave the guilty with grace, and gave His life so that we might live. He emphasized this power by declaring the first and greatest commandment: "Love the Lord your God with all your heart and with all your soul and with all your mind." And the second is like it: "Love your neighbor as yourself." (Matthew 22:37–39)

In this chapter, we explore how love is not just a feeling, but the very foundation of divine power. It is the fuel behind every miracle, the force behind every healing, and the heartbeat of every act of faith. To love as Jesus loves is to tap into a power far greater than anything the world can offer. And when we embrace that kind of love—fully, fiercely, and faithfully—we become vessels of God's presence on earth.

The Gift of Eternal Life

In Matthew 16:22, Peter overwhelmed by sorrow and confusion, took Jesus aside and rebuked Him, saying, *"Far be it from you, Lord; this shall never happen to you!"*

The idea that their beloved Teacher must suffer and die was unthinkable to the disciples. Yet Jesus knew His purpose. On the night of His arrest, He reminded them with eternal clarity in John 14:6, "I am the way, the truth, and the life: no one comes to the Father except through Me."

On the day of His trial, TRUTH stood face to face with Pontius Pilate. Though fully aware that the verdict would be death, Jesus remained silent, surrendered, and steadfast— because only through the Cross and His resurrection on the third day could the penalty for sin be paid in full. He didn't resist. He chose the Cross.

For 33 years, Jesus walked this earth performing miracles, teaching the good news, healing the broken, and fulfilling prophecy — all to rescue humanity and restore the relationship between man and God. This is the power of Divine Love in action.

The Ultimate Sacrifice

He paid the ultimate ransom—giving His life on the old rugged Cross—so that mankind could receive the gift of eternal life. Through the unmatched grace and endless mercy of God, His divine plan for salvation was freely extended to all who believe.

Because of Jesus, death was defeated, hope was restored, and the door to eternity was opened. And here's the truth we celebrate: No one loses when God uses His power. No one is ever the same when touched by the stuff He uses.

Let this truth take root in your heart—Divine Power is still at work today. Believe it. Receive it. Live it.

IV

Living in the Power of the Word

"For the word of God is alive and active. Sharper than any double-edged sword, it penetrates even to dividing soul and spirit, joints and marrow; it judges the thoughts and attitudes of the heart."

– Hebrews 4:12

Divine Healing for Today

Divine Healing is a life-changing journey into the miraculous power of God that still moves today. Rooted in scripture and filled with faith-building truth, this book explores how God uses natural elements, divine timing, and unshakable love to bring restoration to the body, mind, and soul.

From the healing of lepers and the feeding of the 5,000 to the quiet moments of faith where God meets us in our pain. Divine Healing is both a testimony and a guide—reminding readers that miracles are not confined to the pages of the Bible. They are happening now. With every chapter, you'll gain a deeper understanding of God's character, His methods, and most importantly, His desire to see His children whole.

Whether you're believing for a breakthrough or simply seeking to grow your faith, this book will inspire you to trust in the power of God—because healing still happens.

God's Word is not the Ending- His Word is your Beginning.

You've just walked through the miracles of creation, the movement of God through the elements, and the unmatched healing power of Jesus Christ. You've seen how from the very beginning, God used His voice to shape the earth—and how He continues to use nature, people, and even pain to shape you. Every miracle, every moment, every mountain, and every valley is a reminder: God is still moving.

The same God who parted seas, raised the dead, fed thousands, and healed the broken—dwells within you. His power is not just ancient history. It's alive. It's present. And it's personal. You are not just reading about Divine Power; you are invited to walk in it. Every day.

Let this book be more than just a collection of stories—let it be a call to action. Seek His Word daily. Trust His timing. Pay attention to His signs in the wind, the rain, the earth, and your own body. Let the natural world remind you of His supernatural love.

When you feel overwhelmed, remember: you were created with divine purpose, designed for divine power, and destined for divine impact. You are a living testimony in progress. So rise up. Step out in faith. And never forget—God's power is not only around you; it's within you.

Keep walking. Keep trusting. And may you always live in the fullness of His healing, His promises, and His power.

— Faith Word Healing

Heavenly Father,

*We pray that this book will be a blessing
to all. That your reservoir of anointing will
heal every reader and meet their needs.
In Jesus name we pray, Amen!*

More from
Faith Word Healing

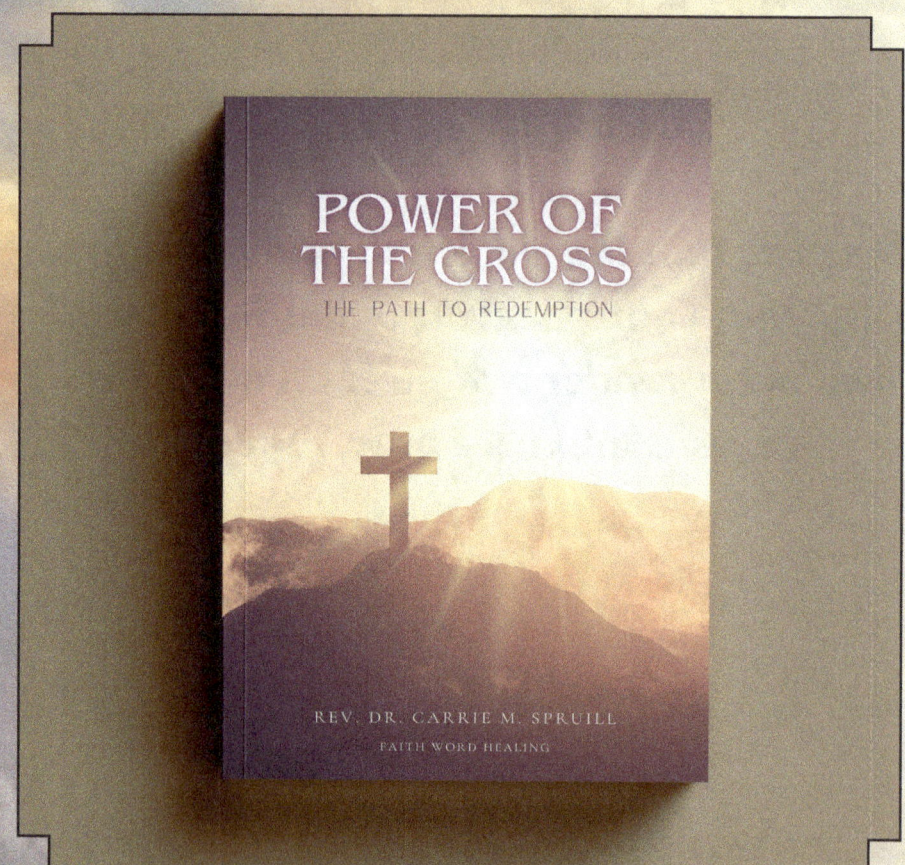

About The Author

Rev. Dr. Carrie M. Spruill is a dynamic speaker and visionary leader, renowned as the founder of Faith Word Healing Ministries, Faith Word Healing Magazine, Sunday Messages, Faithful Talk Podcast, and Power of the Cross.

From a young age, Rev. Dr. Spruill exhibited a remarkable gift for teaching and healing, guided by the presence of the Holy Spirit in her life. By the age of twelve, she was already leading adult Sunday school classes, and by sixteen, she delivered her first public speech at a Baptist Convention.

With a deep reverence for God's Word and a passion for biblical truth, Rev. Dr. Spruill has devoted her life to studying scripture, earning multiple academic degrees including doctorates, master's, and bachelor's degrees—alongside two law degrees. Her insight brings clarity to the divine power displayed through Jesus' crucifixion. She notes Jesus' death was twofold. First, His death was an act of God prophesized in the book of (Isaiah, Chapter 53). Secondly, the Roman governor did not believe Jesus was guilty, but out of fear for his position let the people decide to bring charges to crucify Him (Mark 14:43 -72, and Chapter 15).

Divine Power traces moments like these to uncover how God's might moves through history, prophecy, and everyday life, inviting readers to witness His hand at work.

Drawing from her deep spiritual insight and worldly knowledge, Rev. Dr. Spruill is dedicated to empowering others to fulfill their God-given purposes.

Guided by the belief expressed in Jeremiah 1:5, she endeavors to help individuals recognize and embrace the divine plan mapped out for them before their birth.

www.ingramcontent.com/pod-product-compliance
Lightning Source LLC
Chambersburg PA
CBHW071210120626
46546CB00006B/2502